Dangerous Animals

Rebecca Gilpin

Designed by Will Dawes, Katrina Fearn,
Michelle Lawrence and Zoe Waring
Illustrated by Patrizia Donaera

Additional illustrations by Tim Haggerty
Reading consultant: Alison Kelly, Roehampton University
Animal consultant: Professor Stuart West, University of Edinburgh

Contents

3 Watch out...

4 Stay away!

6 Hunting for food

8 Teamwork

10 After dark

12 Hidden dangers

14 Fast and furious

16 Big bruisers

18 Shark attack

20 Scary seas

22 Vicious venom

24 Don't touch!

26 Deadly diseases

28 Animals in danger

30 Glossary of animal words

31 Websites to visit

32 Index

watch out...

Animals can be dangerous for lots of different reasons. They may be scared, hungry or even protecting their family.

This rattlesnake is rattling its scaly tail. It is a warning that it may attack.

Stay away!

Animals can be dangerous when they are protecting their babies or the place where they live.

A mother polar bear looks after her cubs until they can look after themselves.

A male bear tries to attack the cubs. The mother protects them.

She scares the bear away and her cubs are safe for the moment.

Some animals
defend the area
where they live
and hunt. This
area is called
their territory.

Tigers fight other tigers that come into
their territory. Sometimes they fight until
one of them dies.

Hunting for food

Animals that eat meat kill other animals. Some use special skills to catch their prey.

Cheetahs sprint after prey such as antelopes and then pull them to the ground.

Brown bears wait in streams to catch leaping salmon.

A boa constrictor coils around its prey and squeezes it to death.

A tiger's stripes are like camouflage – it can sneak up on its prey without being seen.

An eagle swoops and snatches a fish in its sharp claws.

Scorpions sting and stun prey with poison in their tails.

Teamwork

Some animals live in groups and hunt as a team, so that they can kill bigger animals.

Wolves live and hunt in family groups called packs. They kill animals such as deer and moose.

Wolves can follow the smell of their prey through the snow.

Female lions hunt together.
They chase a zebra away
from its herd and drag
it to the ground.

One lion bites the
zebra's throat and
holds on until it
stops breathing.

The lions all feed
on the dead zebra.

After dark

When night falls, some animals have special ways of finding prey in the dark.

A pit viper has two deep holes in its face that feel heat given off by other animals.

This means that small animals can't even hide from the viper in the dark.

An owl's large eyes
let it see really well,
even when there is
almost no light.

They fly quietly, then swoop and grab small
animals in their sharp claws.

Hidden dangers

Some animals hide and wait for prey, instead of chasing it.

Leopards climb trees, then leap down onto animals that pass by.

A crocodile swims in a river, with only part of its head showing.

A gazelle drinks from the river but doesn't see the crocodile.

The crocodile lunges up and grabs the gazelle in its jaws.

It rolls over and pulls the gazelle under the water to drown it.

Fast and furious

Some animals move very fast when they are hunting or if something surprises them.

A peregrine falcon spots a pigeon and dives down to attack it.

It crashes into the pigeon at an amazing speed and kills it.

The falcon eats the dead pigeon on the ground.

A hunting cheetah can run three times faster than the fastest person.

Bears can run very fast. They sometimes chase people who catch them by surprise.

Big bruisers

Big animals can be dangerous because of their size and strength.

Hippos are huge. They sometimes kill people who come too close.

Hippos lie in rivers to keep cool.

Male hippos often fight over territory. They attack with their huge teeth.

African elephants are the biggest animals
that live on land. They often charge at
other animals to scare them away.

Shark attack

Sharks are the fiercest hunters in the sea. They can hear and smell prey from a long way away.

Great white sharks hunt big fish, seals and dolphins. Sometimes they attack people too, but this is rare.

This great white shark is breaking through the surface of the sea to attack a seal.

Tiger sharks
have a very good
sense of smell.

A tiger shark smells blood coming from an
injured turtle.

The shark attacks. It crunches the turtle with
its strong jaws and sharp teeth.

Scary seas

Sharks aren't the only killers in the sea. Lots of other dangerous creatures live there too.

A blue-ringed octopus is only as big as a golf ball, but its poison can kill a person in minutes.

It turns bright yellow with blue markings when it is about to attack.

Box jellyfish sting
small fish to death with
their tentacles. Their sting
can also kill people.

A stonefish has poisonous
spines along its back.
It can kill people who
step on it by accident.

Electric rays hide in
the sand and give
an electric shock
if they are touched.

Cone snails inject fish with deadly
poison, then swallow them whole.

Vicious Venom

Some snakes and spiders have sharp fangs filled with poisonous venom. Their venom can be very dangerous to people.

Spitting cobras shoot venom at an attacker's eyes to blind it...

...then they strike with their fangs and inject more deadly venom.

A Sydney funnel-web spider sits inside its web and waits for prey to pass by.

A beetle steps on a thread linked to the web, and the spider feels the web move.

The spider scuttles out. It sinks its fangs into the beetle and injects venom into it.

Don't touch!

Some animals have bright markings or sharp spines that tell other animals to stay away.

The bright skin of a poison arrow frog warns attackers that it is deadly poisonous.

Some people in South America use poison from frogs on their arrows when they go hunting.

Lionfish
have spines
with poison
on the ends.

They swim in the
sea around coral
reefs looking for
small fish to eat.

Sometimes a diver
touches a lionfish by
accident and gets
stung by its spines.

Deadly diseases

Some animals are dangerous because they spread diseases.

A few female mosquitoes can spread a deadly disease called malaria when they bite people.

This mosquito is drinking a person's blood through its straw-like mouth.

Rats live in most places where people live. They carry diseases that can make people very ill.

People can catch diseases from rats' droppings, or from their fleas.

Some flies spread germs by walking on droppings, then landing on people's food.

Animals in danger

People can be even more dangerous to animals than animals are to people.

Hunters shoot and kill wild animals for their fur, skins and horns.

People cut down trees in the places where animals live, and use the land for houses and farming.

Sharks, fish and seabirds are killed by oil leaking from damaged ships.

Plastic bags, cans and bottles can choke animals that try to eat them.

Some people hunt and kill dangerous animals such as sharks for fun.

Many animals are in danger of dying out unless people change some of the things they do.

Glossary of animal words

Here are some of the words in this book you might not know. This page tells you what they mean.

 hunt - to look for, catch and kill animals, usually to eat.

 territory - an area where an animal lives and hunts.

 prey - animals that are hunted and eaten by other animals.

 poisonous - something poisonous can make you ill or kill you.

 venom - a poisonous liquid that some animals use to stun and kill.

 fangs - sharp pointed teeth. Some animals' fangs are filled with venom.

 tentacles - long parts of a jellyfish that can sting and even kill.

Websites to visit

You can visit exciting websites to find out more about dangerous animals.

To visit these websites, go to the Usborne Quicklinks Website at **www.usborne-quicklinks.com** Read the internet safety guidelines, and then type the keywords "**beginners dangerous animals**".

The websites are regularly reviewed and the links in Usborne Quicklinks are updated. However, Usborne Publishing is not responsible, and does not accept liability, for the content or availability of any website other than its own. We recommend that children are supervised while on the internet.

Scorpions come out at night and hunt for bugs.

Index

bears, 4, 6, 15
birds, 7, 11, 14, 28
bugs, 7, 22, 23, 26, 27, 31
cheetahs, 6-7, 15
crocodiles, 12-13
elephants, 17
fangs, 22, 23, 30
fish, 6, 7, 18, 21, 25, 28
hippos, 16
hunting, 5, 6-7, 8-9, 10-11,
    12-13, 14, 15, 18, 19, 24,
    28, 30
leopards, 12-13
lions, 9

people, 15, 16, 18, 20, 21,
    22, 24, 25, 26, 27, 28-29
poison, 7, 20, 21, 22, 23,
    24, 25, 30
prey, 6, 7, 8, 10, 11, 12-13,
    14, 18, 19, 21, 23, 30
rats, 27
sharks, 18-19, 20, 28, 29
snakes, 3, 6, 10, 22, 23
tentacles, 21, 30
territory, 5, 16, 30
tigers, 5, 7
venom, 22-23, 30
wolves, 8

Acknowledgements

Photographic manipulation by John Russell

Photo credits

The publishers are grateful to the following for permission to reproduce material:
© **Alamy** 1 (Steve Bloom Images), 11 (Eureka), 17 (Steve Bloom Images),
18 (Fabrice Bettex), 19 (Stephen Frink Collection), 25 (Ron Steiner); © **Ardea** 12-13 (M. Watson);
© **CORBIS** 5 (John Conrad), 8 (Jeff Vanuga), 24 (Buddy Mays); © **Digital Vision** Cover, 22, 31;
© **Getty Images** 2-3 (National Geographic), 6-7 (Steve Bloom), 15 (Johnny Johnson),
27 (John Downer); © **Natural Visions** 20 (John Lewis); © **Nature Picture Library**
29 (Jeff Rotman); © **Science Photo Library** 26 (Sinclair Stammers).

Every effort has been made to trace and acknowledge ownership of copyright. If any rights have
been omitted, the publishers offer to rectify this in any subsequent editions following notification.

Vikings

Castles

How flowers grow

Knights

Living in space

Caterpillars and Butterflies

Ballet

Pirates

Egyptians

Eggs and Chicks

Romans

Weather

Tadpoles and frogs

Why do we eat?

Under the sea

Bears